C0 APK 951

the **7 dynamos** of organizational **power**™

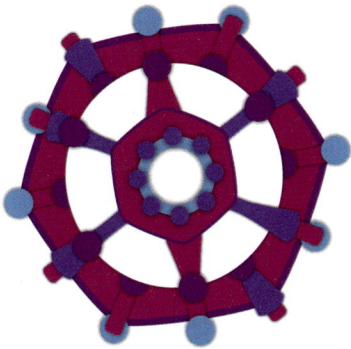

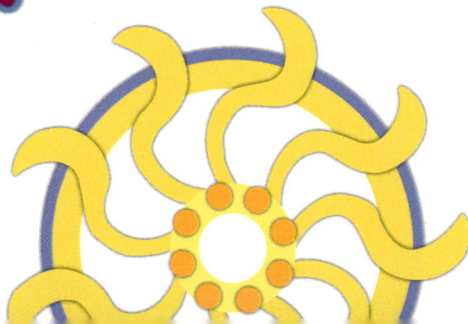

boldly go

ClearSight Technologies, Inc.

COLLEEN CAYES

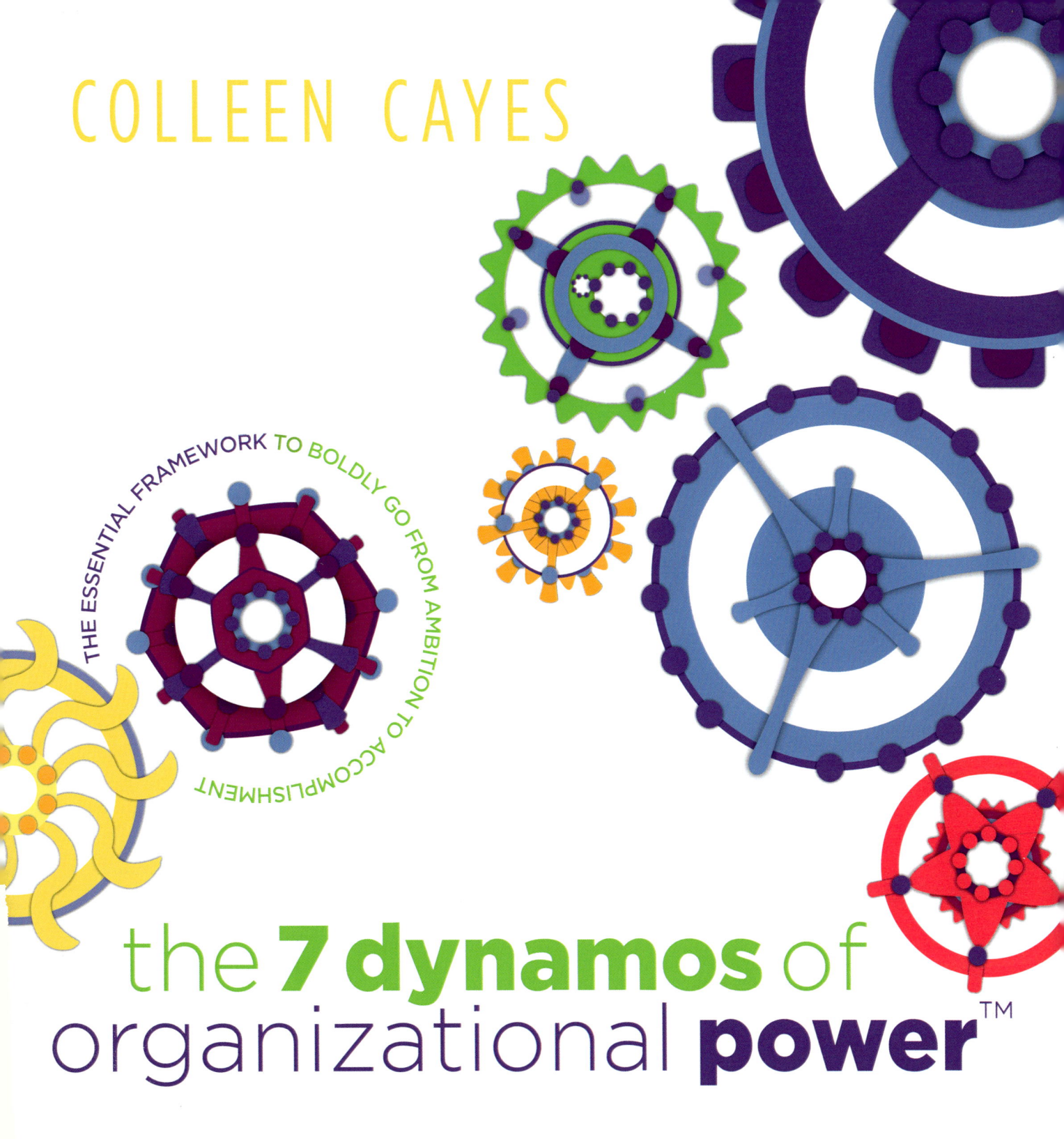

THE ESSENTIAL FRAMEWORK TO BOLDLY GO FROM AMBITION TO ACCOMPLISHMENT

the **7 dynamos** of
organizational **power**™

All text, tables and concepts Copyright © 2020 Colleen Cayes

All rights reserved. Printed in the United States of America.
No part of this publication may be reproduced, stored in a retrieval system,
or transmitted in any manner without written permission except
for brief quotations for review purposes only.

The 7 Dynamos of Organizational Power™ is published by
ClearSight Technologies | Bluff, Utah

Art direction, design and illustration: ïtäl art by Mariah Fox | mariahfox.com
Photo of Colleen on page 94 by Kinya Nippa

For more information:
Colleen Cayes
President, ClearSight Technologies, Inc.
colleen@7dynamos.com
(505) 603-8003
7dynamos.com

ISBN 13: 978-0-578-71918-4
First Edition
10 9 8 7 6 5 4 3 2 1

DEDICATED TO

Stephen R. Covey

Who inspired me by researching
and documenting *The 7 Habits
of Highly Effective People*
...and encouraging "the choice
to lead" in *The 8th Habit*

Alan Mulally

Who showed us all how it's done
as CEO of Ford Motor Company

Clayton M. Christensen

My cherished classmate, who
embodied generosity of spirit

preface

This concise book will show you how to measure and manage ***The 7 Dynamos of Organizational Power.*** It's the "magic decoder ring" for fully claiming your organization's highest potential.

Understanding this simple, actionable framework is like coming around a corner in a racecar and seeing a straightaway ahead. Finally, you will know exactly how to dramatically accelerate your entire organization's success!

Acceleration is not optional. We operate in a world where everyone else is also striving to be hyper-capable. World championship Formula One racing teams win by 2/100th of a second. *The 7 Dynamos of Organizational Power* will give you an edge by showing you how to

1. Consciously and deliberately fine tune each of ***The 7 Dynamos*** for maximum power.

2. Transfer this ability to your team, so you can focus on strategy and growth.

3. Direct your personal reading for greatest impact from hundreds of well-researched and insightful books, articles, and TED Talks. [1]

This book is designed to be quick to read. Each ***Dynamo*** will be familiar. You have certainly experienced all of them, in their positive or negative expressions, during your career. Where they were strong and pulling together, it was exciting and fulfilling to go to work. Where they were weak or absent, you felt frustrated, demoralized, disconnected.

[1] Bibliography at www.7dynamos.com

You'll see right away where to put the insights of The 7 Dynamos into action. Helpful tools are listed in Part III of this book, and you can find more resources at www.7dynamos.com.

table of contents

&& The best way to
predict the future
is to create it."

- Peter Drucker

WHAT IS ORGANIZATIONAL POWER?

Organizational power is the ability to set and achieve ambitious goals.

Organizational power is SpaceX doing the "absurd, dangerous, impossible" by landing and re-using its rocket's first stage.

It is scrappy little Southwest Airlines growing to be number one in US skies. It is Steve Jobs' "one more thing" becoming the *must-have* new product all over the world.

Organizational power is making the right strategic decisions for the future while delivering with excellence for today's customers.

Organizational power is the "secret sauce" that makes customers, suppliers, employees, and investors believe in you.

Building a powerful organization requires skill and creativity, with as many expressions as there have been bosses since organizational life began. As the builder of your own organization, you shape its visible presentation to the world.

This book peels back the surface to reveal the essential internal framework that all organizations share, like the invisible steel ribs of skyscrapers. Deep inside, giving organizations the muscle to grow and achieve great goals, are *The 7 Dynamos of Organizational Power.*

WHERE DOES ORGANIZATIONAL POWER COME FROM?

Organizational power is generated by The 7 Dynamos. Each contributes its own force and energy. All are required. As a system, they boost each other to deliver maximum organizational power.

I have labeled them *Dynamos* because they generate momentum, energy, and forward motion like spinning turbines. If any is missing or weak, the organization will be underpowered. A combustion engine loses power if one cylinder loses compression or the valve timing is off. The Dynamos must all operate together at maximum strength for the organization to feel "turbocharged."

The 7 Dynamos framework had its genesis in 2010, when I started searching for the reasons some of my consulting clients were wildly successful, and others were not. It seemed to me that I was applying the same level and quality of expertise. I didn't understand why their results could be so different. I wrote clues for myself on Post-it Notes® and stuck them above my desk. I began to recognize that certain clients had something recognizable as "organizational power," and others did not. I wondered why? what exactly is it? How do companies or other organizations get it, keep it, and measure and manage it?

In the summer of 2015, my observations coalesced into *The 7 Dynamos of Organizational Power*. By then, I had first-hand confirmation that managing these essential drivers could dramatically accelerate an organization's success.[2] And I had proven that eight **Power-Process Tools** could correct weaknesses and turbocharge The 7 Dynamos.

Stephen R. Covey (*The 7 Habits of Highly Effective People,* 1989) and Napoleon Hill (*Think and Grow Rich,* 1934) famously researched and documented what they insisted were "timeless, universal, self-evident principles" of personal success. The 7 Dynamos of Organizational Power are the universal principles of group success.

[2] Success Stories at www.7dynamos.com

WHY IS ORGANIZATIONAL POWER ESSENTIAL?

We all recognize companies that have organizational power because they regularly announce ambitious goals and meet them. And, alas, we mourn formerly admired icons like HP and GE, who somehow lost their organizational mojo.

Ambitious goals are ones that put you out in front of the pack. Whether you're expanding market share, securing customer loyalty, or building commitment to a cause, your organization is in a race.

Winning the race requires two forms of acceleration — speed and agility.

Speed is arriving at the finish line faster. Speed requires control to avoid costly mistakes, and control requires discipline to act in a strategically coherent way.

Agility is arriving at the right finish line. Agility is recognizing when the destination or the paths to get there must change in some way for the organization to win.

When an organization's 7 Dynamos are strong, they generate both speed and agility. For example, a visionary **Leader** recognizes and acts on changes in the environment; competent **People** feel safe bringing up challenging ideas in a **Culture** of trust and transparency; **Structure** and **Process** do not stifle change through bureaucracy.

The 7 Dynamos are essential for all kinds of organizations — businesses, not-for-profits, educational and military administrations, and research and government bodies. Each will differ by the functions in its org chart, yet all will share the necessary framework for success of The 7 Dynamos of Organizational Power.

The org chart and the Dynamos represent different types of indispensable capability. Powerful Dynamos unleash the full potential of the org chart.

The 7 Dynamos hold true in every economic season, across geographies, and within all cultures. They are as essential in the Internet Age as they were for the Roman Empire, and we can be confident they will one day underlie the success of the Mars Colony.

SYMPTOMS AND EVIDENCE

Use this simple quiz to quickly assess your organizational power. Check each below that applies.

Symptoms of an Underpowered Organization

- ❑ Declining market share, stagnant revenue or profits
- ❑ Slow pace of innovation, missing commitments to customers
- ❑ Poor product performance, quality problems
- ❑ Deteriorating financial strength, increased leverage, downgraded bond rating
- ❑ Finger-pointing, morale and retention problems
- ❑ Inadequate technical or managerial bench strength
- ❑ Recognized need for a turnaround

Evidence of Organizational Power

- ❑ Leading / increasing market valuation
- ❑ Leading / growing market share
- ❑ Customer loyalty, strong brand
- ❑ Clear sense of direction, pride in performance, employees feel empowered
- ❑ Internal talent ready to be promoted, high performers want to join
- ❑ Predictable performance on commitments to clients and partners
- ❑ Deep financial resources for R&D, capital, acquisitions

Symptoms and Evidence of organizational power are readily apparent in an organization's market power, product power, and people and financial strength. Turn the page to understand the role of The 7 Dynamos in "draining, sustaining, or gaining" organizational power.

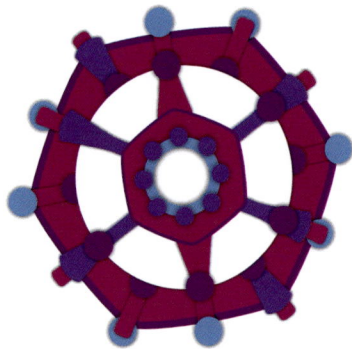

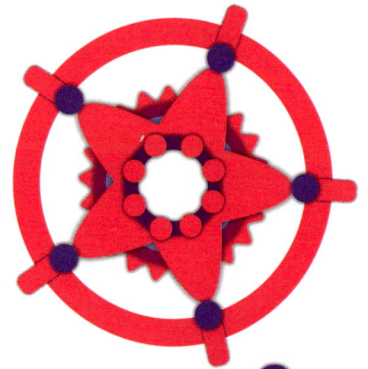

Victory is beyond the power of any individual, and yet is absolutely dependent on the strength of the individual leader."

- Gregory R. Copley

The Art of Victory: Strategies for Personal Success and Global Survival in a Changing World, 2006

HOW THE 7 DYNAMOS GENERATE ORGANIZATIONAL POWER

1. Leader Dynamo

The master gear that regulates the momentum of all the others

2. Purpose Dynamo

The defined course for claiming the organization's potential value

3. Structure and Process Dynamo

The invisible turbochargers of organizational design

4. Management Dynamo

The generator of stability and productivity over time

5. Culture Dynamo

The force multiplier of shared values and behaviors

6. People Dynamo

The leading indicator

7. Resources Dynamo

The managed relationships with external ecosystems

the **7 dynamos** of organizational **power**™

T he 7 Dynamos fit together like cogs spinning in a high-precision machine. Each is always either adding to organizational power, just idling, or outright stalling it.

The **Leader** Dynamo is the heart of the system, motivating and regulating the power of the others. Without that active center, the other Dynamos cannot sustain coherent momentum.

The **Purpose** Dynamo comes alive as the Leader articulates the vision and strategies. **Structure and Process** are the design for organized action.

The **Management** Dynamo keeps the daily action aligned with the Purpose. The **Culture** Dynamo reinforces the internal consistency of decisions and behaviors.

The **People** Dynamo is the source of talent, creativity, decision making, and "elbow grease." The organization manages relationships with external **Resources** to create value.

When all 7 Dynamos are vigorously engaged, the organization can accelerate its journey from ambition to accomplishment, confident of victory in its chosen arena.

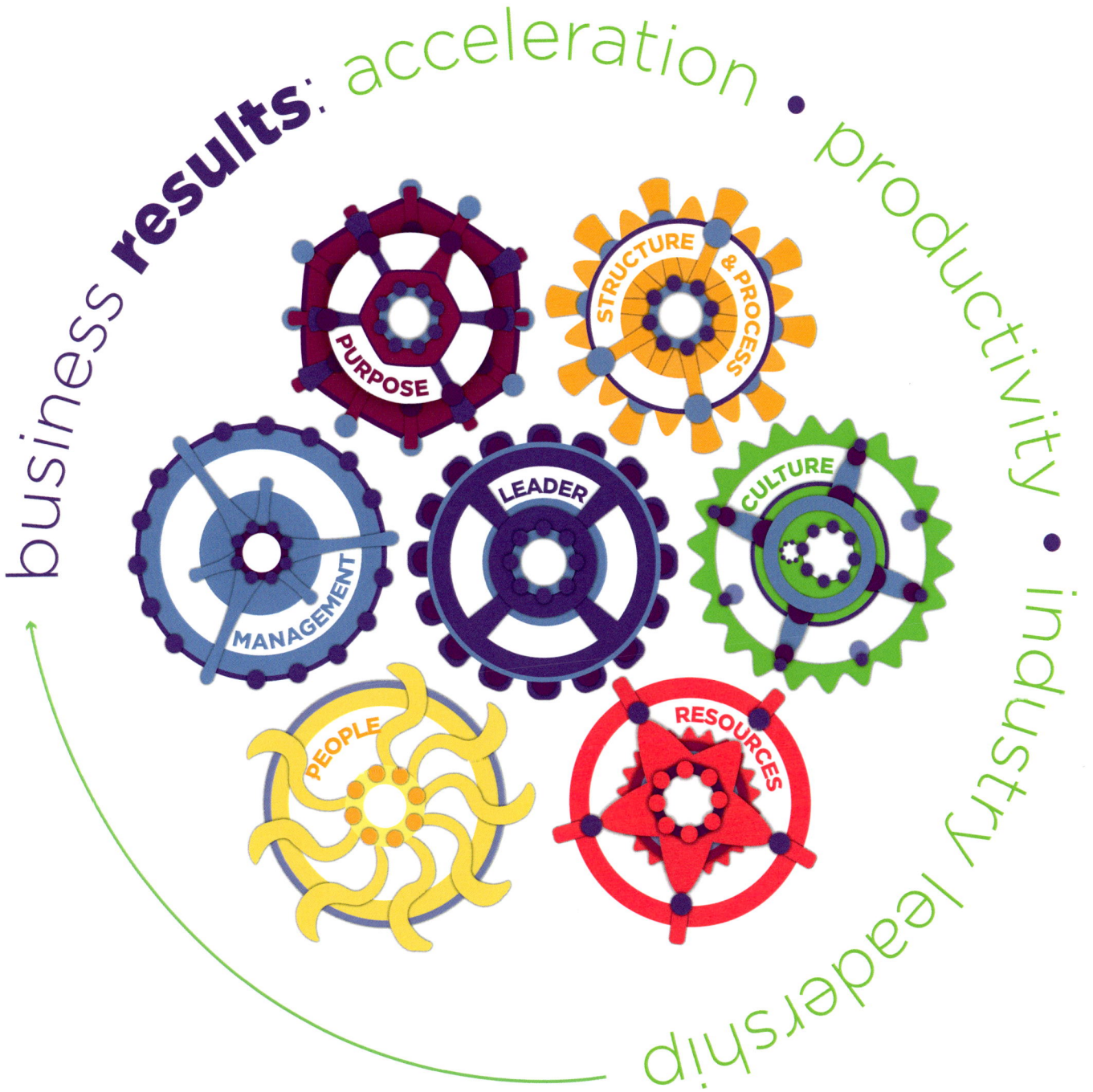

business **results**: acceleration • productivity • industry leadership

PURPOSE

STRUCTURE & PROCESS

MANAGEMENT

LEADER

CULTURE

PEOPLE

RESOURCES

13

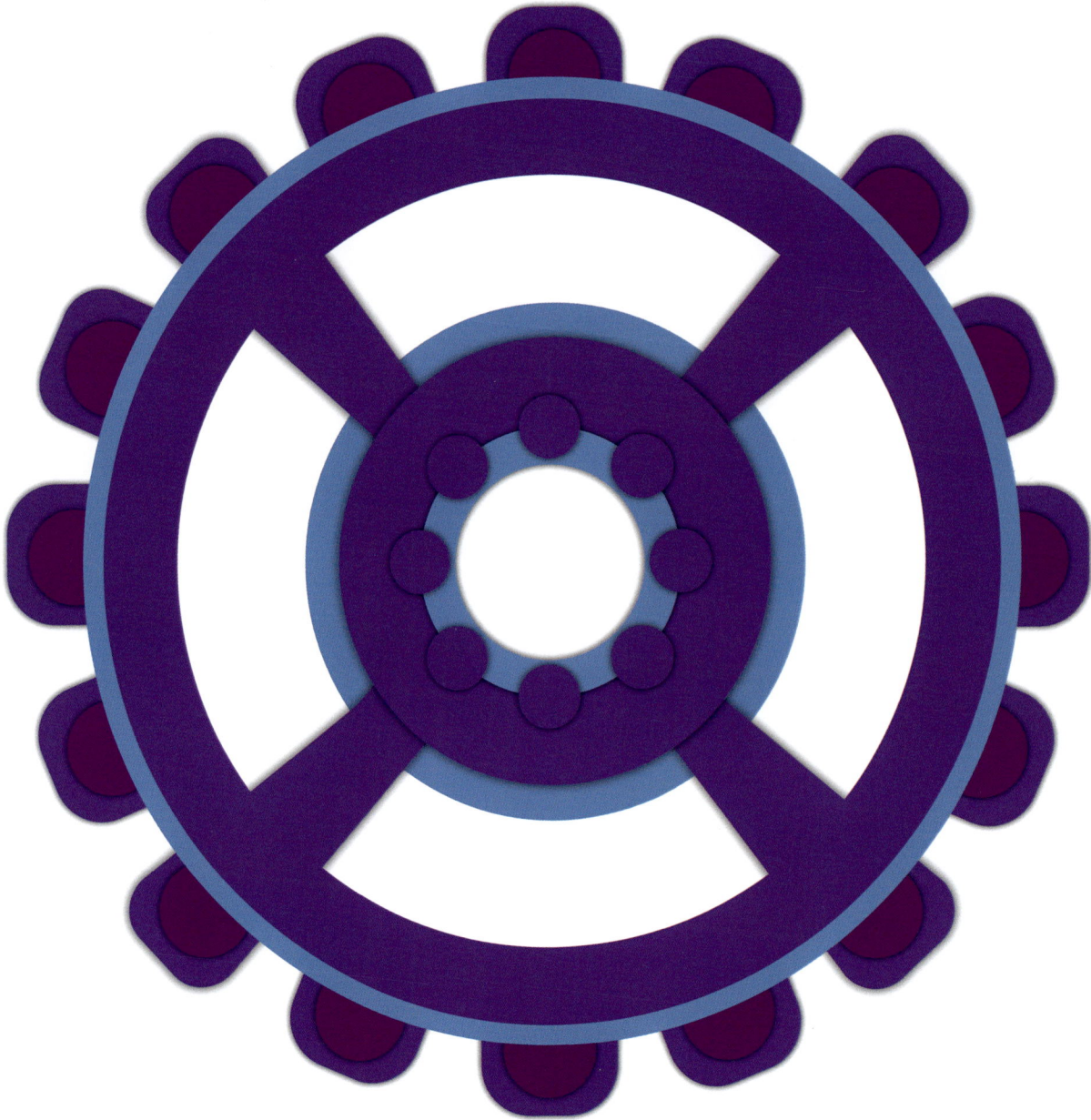

II. HOW THE 7 DYNAMOS GENERATE ORGANIZATIONAL POWER

ESSENTIALS OF THE LEADER DYNAMO

- **Vision**
- **Legitimacy**
- **Integrity**
- **Commitment**
- **Generous Spirit**

1 the leader dynamo

The Leader is the master gear that regulates the momentum of all the others.

Like the driver in a racecar, the Leader provides direction and control to fulfill the organization's potential. A Ferrari in the driveway is just a beautiful sculpture without the driver.

The Leader is the only Dynamo that also appears on the org chart. It is the Leader's responsibility to strengthen the Dynamos to unleash the full potential of the organization's design.

There is no substitute for personal leadership. Leaders are not interchangeable.

Replacing the Leader will change the organization.

Let me describe a client experience that cemented my long-held conviction that this is true. In a two-story industrial building on the east side of Silicon Valley, I watched an organization of 450 engineers, science PhDs, and skilled technicians transform completely because of one person, a new Leader.

Before this new Leader took charge, employees felt fear as they walked towards the front door every morning. It was common for management to humiliate engineers in meetings. The products were late to market and often didn't work; customers didn't want to buy them. It was standard operating procedure to deflect blame instead of taking responsibility.

Six months later, this division had transformed from a toxic workplace into a collaborative and disciplined team. By the end of the year, its products were objectively measured against competing products as the best in the world, and customers were demanding more of them.

What did the new Leader do to bring about this change? Some of it was invisible to people outside the organization. He listened and treated people with respect. He articulated clear goals and a vision for change. He was a role model for trust and collaboration.

Beyond his personal leadership, he also introduced several very visible structured tools and processes. As people used these tools, they built clarity and efficiency, tore down functional silos, and abandoned the blame habit. Everyone signed up for the jointly held inspiring goals and clear action plans. Sister divisions saw the change and adopted the processes and tools.

This was not the first time I had observed the power of the Leader Dynamo in action, but it was certainly the most dramatic. One person had led the complete transformation of 450 people's experience at work through his personal example, commitment to the "heavy lifting" of leadership, clearly articulated vision of the outcomes, and unambiguous generosity of spirit to build up the whole team's confidence and capability.

Alan Mulally said, "Leadership is a design job."[3] He meant more than restructuring the org chart and the product lineup. Less tangible but equally critical can be the need for redesign through the lens of The 7 Dynamos. Mulally designed organizational power back into Ford Motor Company.

In my experience, these five are the essential qualities of Leaders who build organizational power by serving as "the exemplar of a permanent human aspiration — the determination to devote one's powers to jobs worth doing." [4]

FIVE ESSENTIAL QUALITIES OF LEADERS

Vision	Sees ahead to an inspiring destination, a vision that commands attention. Has the courage to challenge the status quo. Embodies the mission.
Legitimacy	Competence, domain mastery. Authority, power. Willingness to accept responsibility. Worthiness to lead.
Integrity	Good character. High standards. Trustworthy. Personal values that strengthen the organization and are the direct source of its culture. Respected as the leader.
Commitment	Insists. Persists. Consistent. Committed to the heavy lifting. Dedicated to leading.
Generous Spirit	Believes in, supports, cares about, mentors, grows others. Recognizes and develops people's potential. Willingness to serve.

[3] *American Icon: Alan Mulally and the Fight to Save Ford Motor Company,* by Bryce G. Hoffman, 2012

[4] *The Concept of Corporate Strategy,* by Kenneth R. Andrews, 1987

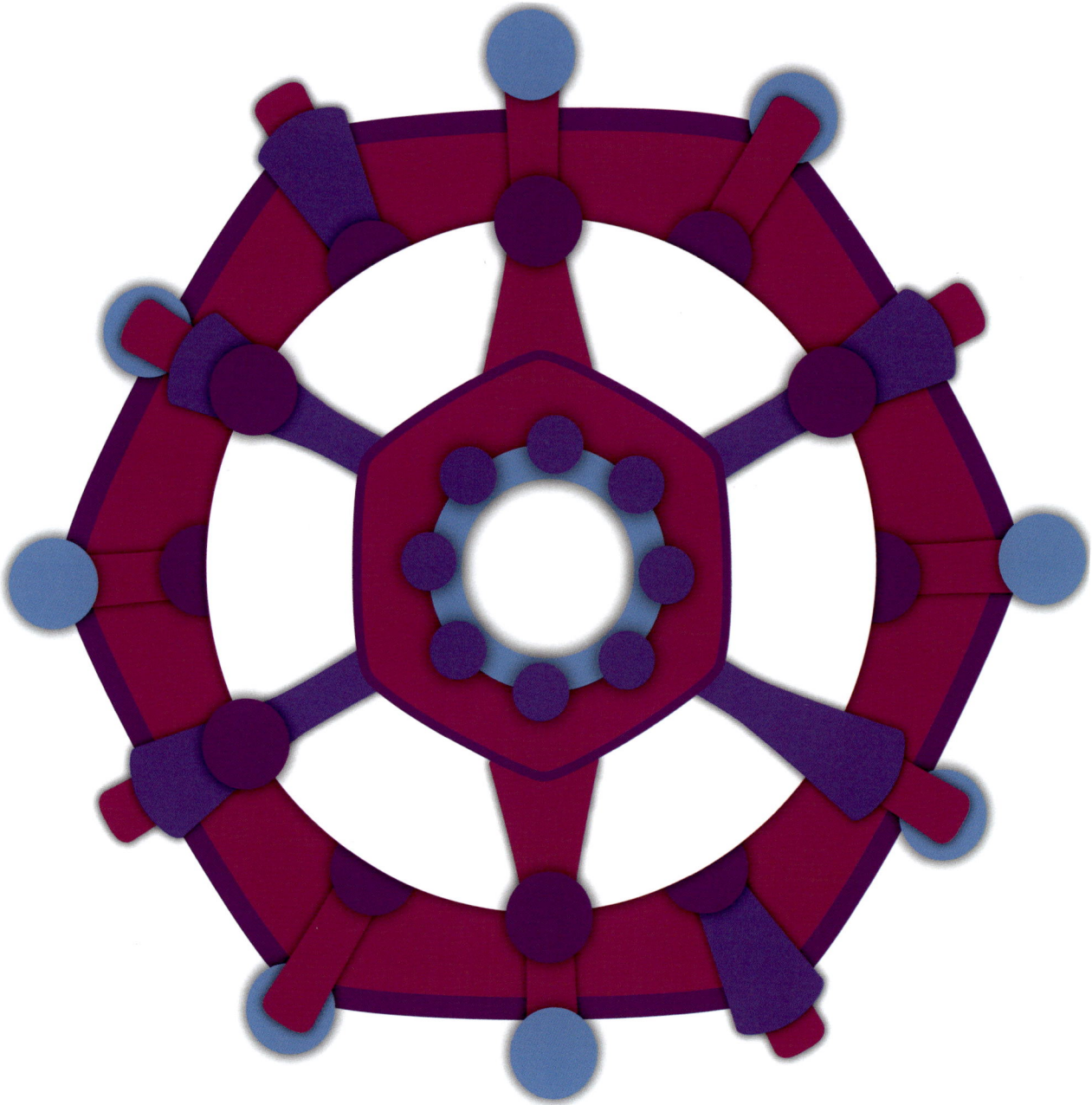

II. HOW THE 7 DYNAMOS GENERATE ORGANIZATIONAL POWER

the purpose dynamo

ESSENTIALS
OF THE
PURPOSE
DYNAMO

- **Vision**
- **Strategy**
- **Mission**
- **Goals**
- **Metrics**

Purpose defines the course an organization will take to claim its potential value.

At full power, the Purpose Dynamo is a set of clearly articulated and communicated "design decisions" that inform every structure, process, decision, and outcome. Specifics morph over time. Strategies change as technologies and customer needs evolve and as the organization judges how much it can influence, vs. adapt to, its environment.

Purpose is the potential value the organization was founded to fulfill. It is Stephen Covey's "begin with the end in mind." It's the "why."

> *"The policy problems of business, like those of policy in public affairs, have to do with the choice of purposes, the development and recognition of organization identity and character, the unending definition of what needs to be done, the mobilization of resources for the attainment of goals in the face of aggressive competition or adverse circumstance, and the definitions of standards for the enforcement of responsible and ethical behavior."* [5]

A turbocharged Purpose Dynamo inspires and drives coherent action by everyone in the organization. It aligns today's decisions with the organization's future goals.

The Leader is responsible not only to help the organization articulate the Purpose; he or she must be seen to personally identify with it. The Leader Dynamo and the Purpose Dynamo share the same essential of Vision.

Organizations gain power by clearly and credibly articulating their Purpose in terms of vision, strategy, mission, goals, and success metrics.

[5] Ibid.

ESSENTIALS OF THE PURPOSE DYNAMO

Vision	The destination: Believing in something that doesn't yet exist; the desire to fulfill potential (creation)
Strategy	The direction: The route(s) that the org has decided will take it to its destination (choices)
Mission	The deliverables: Promises the org makes to its customers and other stakeholders (commitment)
Goals	The outcomes: Specific measurable outcomes in dollars, time, KPI improvements, volumes, etc. (control)
Success Metrics	The distance: Accomplishments relative to the baseline (change)

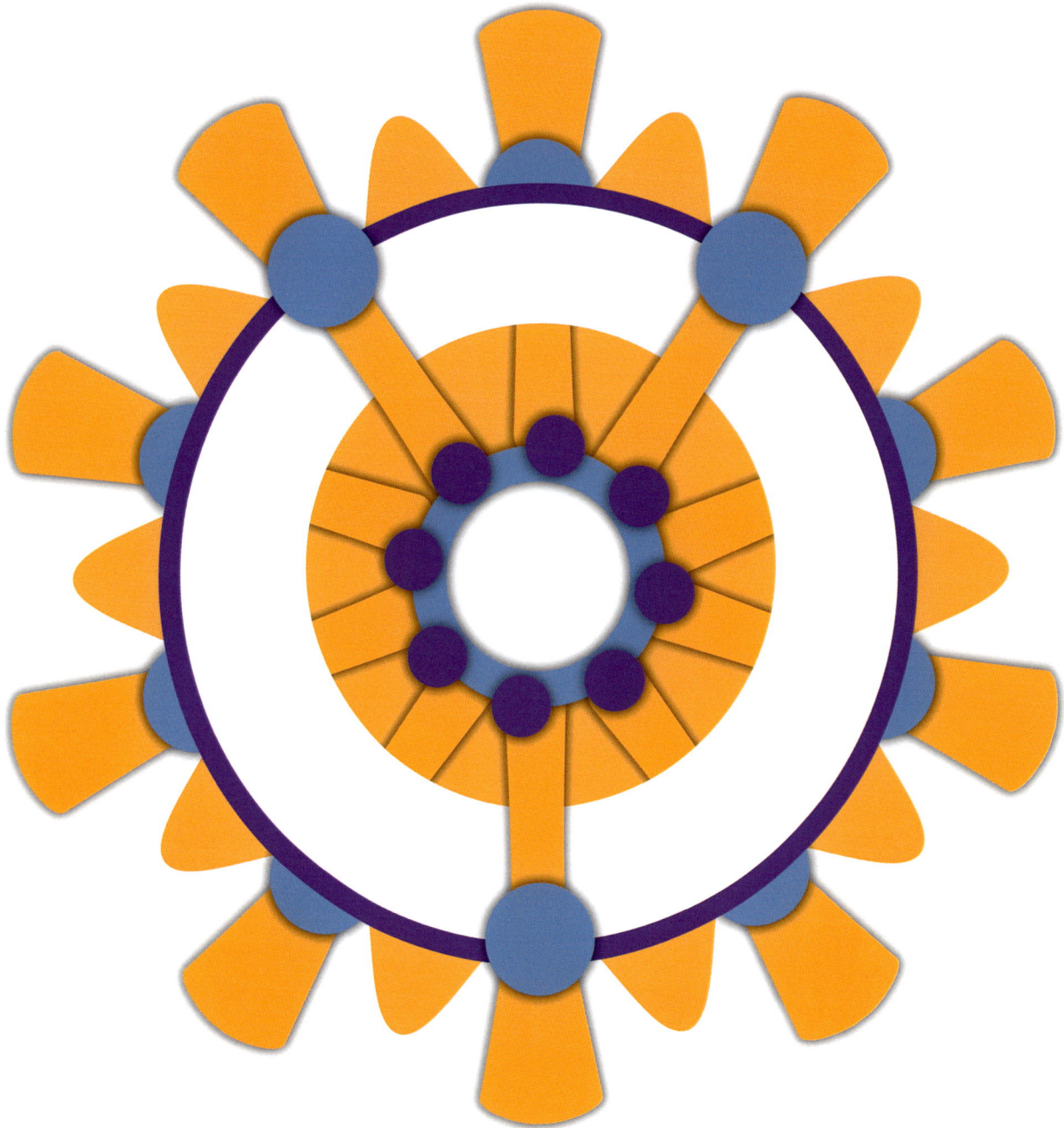

II. HOW THE 7 DYNAMOS GENERATE ORGANIZATIONAL POWER

ESSENTIALS OF THE STRUCTURE AND PROCESS DYNAMO

- **Planning**
- **Organizing**
- **Roles & Responsibilities**
- **Processes**
- **Governance**

3

the structure and process dynamo

Structure and Process are the invisible turbochargers of organizational design.

Like our bones and muscles, Structure and Process are "invisible" enablers of action. Their vital role can be taken for granted in the urgent day-to-day bustle. Structure and Process are not "the work" of the organization. Rather, they are the design for how that work will get done.

Structure is stable; processes are dynamic.

Structure is design through order, like bones. Change the structure, change the range of possible outcomes. Compare the skeleton of a cheetah, built for speed, with that of the more powerful tiger. Structures generally provide long-term form, such as when a company chooses to organize itself by function or by product-focused divisions.

Teams are sub-structures within the organization. They provide temporary or localized flexibility for responding to crises and for initiating and managing innovation. Good teams follow defined processes and norms.

Processes are like muscles, delivering choice of movement. Processes govern productivity. Movements can be fluid and efficient or irregular and wasteful.

Every organization's Structure and Process must be designed with deliberate care to translate its unique intangible Purpose into concrete actions and measurable outcomes. Organization is the key to fulfilling the potential of any organization.[6] Stephen E. Ambrose observed that the rapidity with which the transcontinental railroad was built was possible because of the organizing skills learned during the recently ended Civil War.

President Dwight D. Eisenhower has been widely quoted as saying, "Plans are nothing; planning is everything." Planning is making decisions ahead of time. Good decisions often require analysis, identifying dependencies, and making tradeoffs. All of these take time. As circumstances change, good new decisions can be made more quickly because the options were well understood beforehand.

> *"It is not only possible but also essential to plot a course into a future that cannot be foretold and to develop organization strengths that can keep a company adaptive and make it innovative."* [7]

[6] *Nothing Like it in the World: The Men Who Built the Transcontinental Railroad 1863-1869,* by Stephen E. Ambrose, 2000

[7] *The Concept of Corporate Strategy*, by Kenneth R. Andrews, 1987

Structure and Process are so important that if done wrong, they can bring an organization to a standstill. Optimal Structure and Process encourage disciplined, deliberate action without ossifying into bureaucracy, where form takes precedence over function.[8]

> *"Organizations that operate in silos are not only inefficient; they can also strangle efforts at strategic change. The organization chart becomes a straightjacket. An effective Leader must break down the barriers so all functions work together. The desire to build fiefdoms and protect them is rampant in the military industrial complex, the federal government, and even research universities. Perverse incentives encourage turf battles (e.g., the more direct reports, the higher the manager's pay)."* [9]

To be turbochargers, Structure and Process must also encourage creativity. When rules replace human initiative, they smother it.

> *"The key to growth is entrepreneurial creativity. As Princeton's Albert Hirschman wrote, "Creativity always comes as a surprise to us. If it didn't, we wouldn't need it, and planning would work."* [10]

Victor Davis Hanson has called organization a form of "hard power." Smaller military forces have overcome larger ones with superior organization. The way a business or not-for-profit initiative is structured will have an impact on its success. Investing up front in proper design pays off in greater efficiency, less waste, higher quality, and better managed risk.

---

[8] *Managing Corporate Lifecycles: How Organizations Grow, Age, and Die* by Ichak Kalderon Adizes, 2004

[9] Janet Jacobs, President of Anchor Audio and Discount Audio, 2007-2017

[10] *Knowledge and Power,* by George Gilder, 2013

ESSENTIALS OF THE STRUCTURE & PROCESS DYNAMO

Planning	Deciding in advance, managing the timeline. The British Army's 7P's: *Prior proper planning prevents piss poor performance.* Regularly updated and integrated strategies.
Organizing	Scope. Structure. Definitions. Categories. Visual order, war rooms. Hierarchy, network, hub & spoke, steering council. Org chart. Frameworks, platforms.
Roles & Responsibilities	Clarity about who does what. Lack of confusion = efficiency. Avoids blaming, out of balance workloads, inaction due to ineffective communications. Better morale.
Processes	Business processes, feedback loops, corrective action. Productivity, repeatability. The balance point between order and creativity.
Governance	Ongoing alignment between accountability, incentives, rewards.

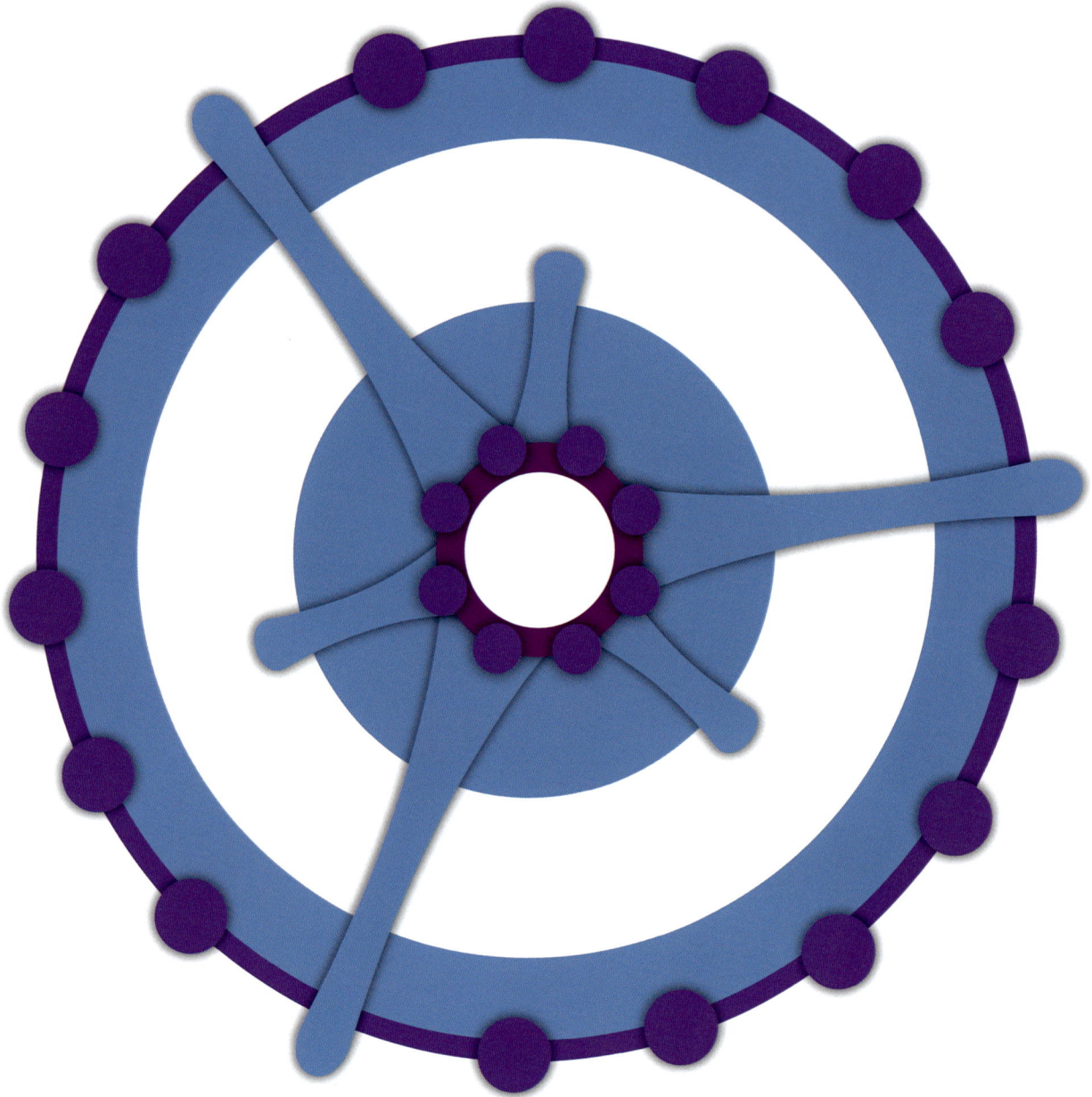

II. HOW THE 7 DYNAMOS GENERATE ORGANIZATIONAL POWER

the management dynamo

> ## ESSENTIALS OF THE MANAGEMENT DYNAMO
>
> - **Prioritize**
> - **Delegate**
> - **Communicate**
> - **Measure**
> - **Control**

The Management Dynamo's role is to generate stability and productivity over time.

Managers make the decisions and corrections that keep the organization on track, like the steering wheel, gas pedal, and brakes of the car.

Like Leaders, Managers deliver outcomes through others. They must delegate work to the right people, measure and report outcomes against the plan, take disciplinary action and give rewards, model behavior consistent with the organization's values, and communicate changes. At a minimum,

Management's oversight is focused on meeting immediate customer needs. At its best, it also assures alignment of today's deliverables with the organization's Purpose.

Managers must generate the right degree of stability without stifling initiative. Employee engagement is a direct source of productivity. In the Manager's hands are the twin levers of morale: communications and control. When people feel they know what's going on and what they are supposed to do, they are willing to give more of themselves to the job.

It is often said that people don't leave a company; they leave their manager. When a Manager properly prioritizes, delegates, communicates, and measures outcomes, giving people the sense that the organization's work is in control and aligned with its Purpose, People are motivated to excel, to take on new growth opportunities, and to remain loyal, long-term contributors.

The great investor, Warren Buffett, recognizes the critical role of Management in profitable growth:

> "Buffett also focuses on management. He doesn't look at a company's CEO, but rather at its deep structure – its culture, its resilience and the manner in which its strategy permeates the day-to-day life of the business. A good company creates good management; good management builds a good company... CEO's retire; heads of departments come and go. The individual making the decisions is not the most important part of the company; the system of decision-making and operations is. These qualities will outlast the individual. You cannot invest in a company for decades based on your admiration for a handful of people." [11]

[11] George Friedman, *Geopolitical Futures, Warren Buffett and Geopolitical Forecasting,* May 8 2017

Management is not the same as leadership. Leadership is a talent, which can be honed and developed. Leadership is about imagination and "getting somewhere new." Management is a profession.[12] It can be learned. Management is about "producing results here and now."

ESSENTIALS OF THE MANAGEMENT DYNAMO

Prioritize	Allocate resources to meet deadlines. Make tradeoffs based on robust decision-making tools and processes.
Delegate	Assign work, oversee progress, facilitate action. Support and develop people. Reinforce clear Roles & Responsibilities and business processes.
Communicate	Listen. Inform. Give and solicit feedback. Set the example. Establish meeting cadence, process, and content. Publish policies. Model organizational values.
Measure	Measure and evaluate results. Establish control systems, metrics, budgets, status reports. Plan-Do-Check-Adjust cycle. Identify areas for improvement. Celebrate successes.
Control	Hold people accountable with consistency and fairness. Follow through on corrective action. Manage rewards, promotions, reassignments, termination.

[12] HBS Bulletin, October 1989, review of the book, *The Managerial Mystique,* by Abraham Zaleznik

II. HOW THE 7 DYNAMOS GENERATE ORGANIZATIONAL POWER

ESSENTIALS OF THE CULTURE DYNAMO

- **Accountable**
- **Transparent**
- **Collaborative**
- **Proactive**
- **Ethical**

5
the culture dynamo

Culture is the force multiplier of shared values and behaviors.

Culture is visible in the decisions, priorities, beliefs, expectations, and behaviors of the organization. An organization's Culture is reinforced by shared history, norms, and language.

A winning culture turbocharges productivity. Put the best People to work in a weak Culture, and they will underperform. Most of us have experienced how a "bad" Culture limited us and a "great" one unleashed our motivation and ability to excel. The brilliantly insightful Ichak Adizes, author of *Managing Corporate Lifecycles,* perceptively said, "A bad culture grinds good people to powder." [13]

[13] Personal communication, 2001

Culture originates in the Leader's character. Switch out that one person, and watch the culture inevitably transform to reflect his or her values. Imagine if Elon Musk (Tesla) and Mary Barra (General Motors) switched places. Would we not anticipate an immediate impact on the culture and performance of both companies?

What makes a Culture bad or good? It depends. Individuals may thrive in one, but not another. The Culture must be a fit with the organization's Purpose. The culture that empowers the US Marine Corps is not as well suited to the people and purpose of the Metropolitan Opera.

For organizations operating in the free enterprise world, a Culture that promotes accountability, transparency, collaboration, initiative, and integrity is designed to win.

I briefly worked for a company whose Culture failed on every one of these metrics. Avoiding accountability had been raised to an art form. I was appalled when my new admin regularly scheduled me to be in three meetings at the same time. After a few weeks, I learned that at least two, if not all three, of the meetings would be canceled by the time the date rolled around. This meant that meetings in which I had committed to an action would not recur, so no one would ever ask if I had followed through. The entire company also reorganized every year, so last year's numbers for any department could not be compared to this year's performance. Brilliant! I experienced the culture as non-transparent, silo'd, reactive, and frequently willing to shade the truth. Interestingly, a number of people had been thriving in that culture for years.

At this same company I learned some excellent Management practices. In spite of that, and some of the most qualified colleagues I've ever worked with, the company's Culture was such a drag on its performance that it was firmly in third place of three in its industry. Its great potential was left unclaimed by the failure of its Culture.

Working there "for one miserable year" sharply confirmed my career-long observations about the Culture Dynamo. I had just left a company where I felt privileged to wear my badge because of its high standards and passion for collaboration. I thus had the invaluable experience of working back-to-back in "the best" culture for me, where the company also led in global market share, and the "worst," where both individual and company performance were hamstrung by a dysfunctional Culture Dynamo.

ESSENTIALS OF THE CULTURE DYNAMO

Accountable	Be responsible. "Do what you say you will do." (DWYSYWD was an original component of "The HP Way," back when Hewlett-Packard was widely admired and imitated). Follow through. *Leader's Character: Disciplined*
Transparent	Be open. Be clear. Share information. Make it safe for constructive conflict. Trust and be trustworthy. *Leader's Character: Truthful*
Collaborative	Build consensus, not competition. Valuing alignment. Emotional commitment, engagement, passion. *Leader's Character: Generous / Inclusive*
Proactive	Take initiative to solve, predict, and avoid problems and capture opportunities. Don't tolerate passive aggressive behavior. *Leader's Character: Responsible*
Ethical	Be honest. Leverage Stephen M.R. Covey's "speed of trust" internally and with customers and suppliers. Reputation leverage, social capital. *Leader's Character: Principled*

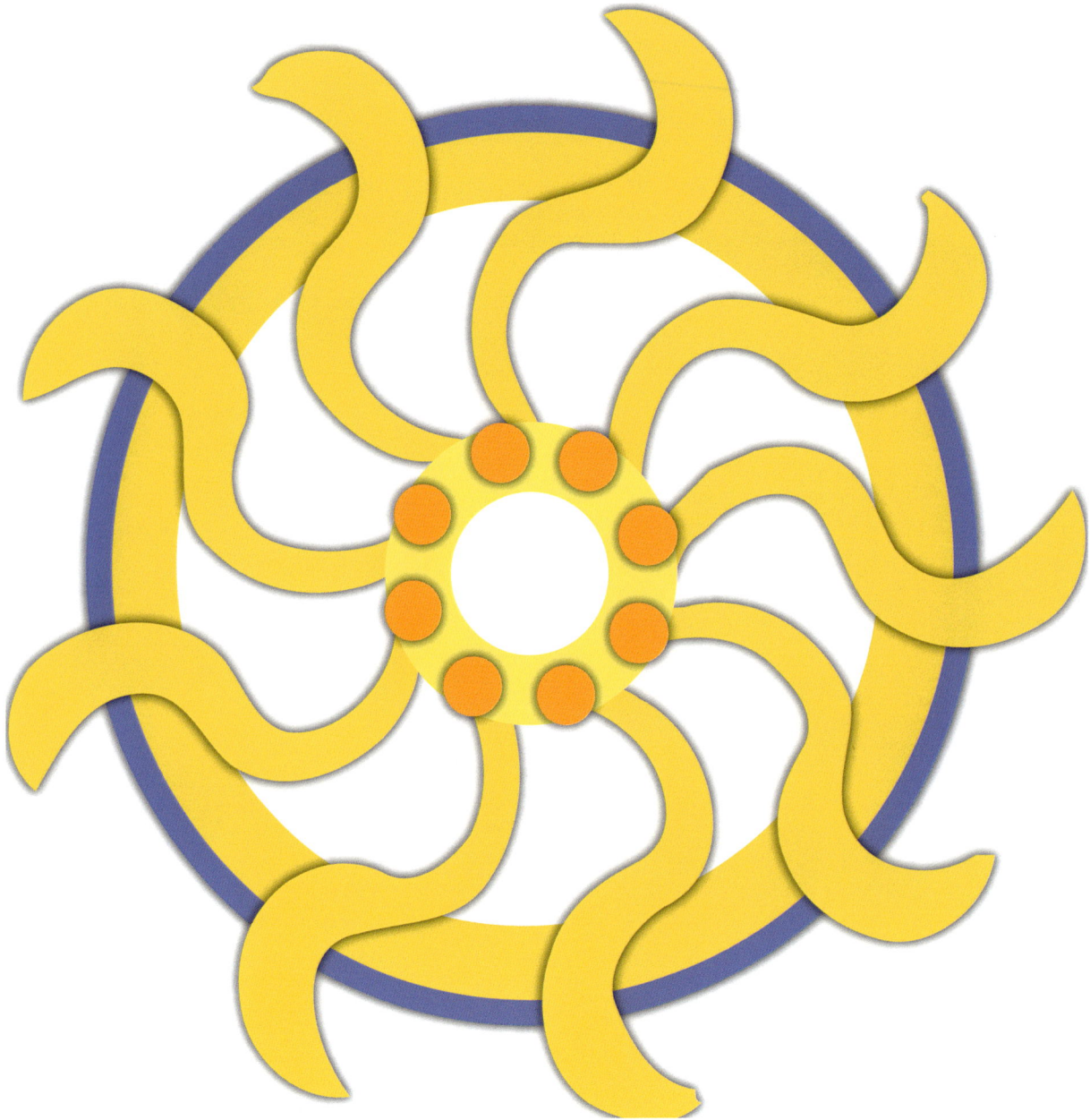

II. HOW THE 7 DYNAMOS GENERATE ORGANIZATIONAL POWER

ESSENTIALS OF THE PEOPLE DYNAMO

- **Job Skills**
- **Bandwidth**
- **Experience**
- **Maturity**
- **Advancement Readiness**

6
the people dynamo

The People Dynamo is the leading indicator.

I once had a white board at the office, and every day I added names of the company's top performers who were resigning to seek greater opportunity. I knew this was a danger sign, and sure enough, within about a year, the company was being acquired by a competitor.

An organization requires people to come together for a particular Purpose. Without the People, you may have a great idea, a terrific Leader, legal documents and a bank account, but you have no capacity for coordinated action. The People Dynamo is the source of the organization's relationships, creativity, execution, growth, profitability, and reputation — everything that brings Purpose to life.

Jim Collins says an organization must have "the right people on the bus." The right people are measured by more than job descriptions on file with HR. The talent, skills, and experience to productively do today's work are critical; so is the ability for people to grow and adapt to changes in an organization's size, challenges, and even its Purpose over time. Capabilities may need to change with technology and expansion. The number of people may expand or contract with a redesign of the business model. New or different types of people may be required to address different demographic markets or geographies.

You start by hiring the right people.

> *If building teams is the most important function for a Manager, then hiring is critical to the organization's success. Too often this function is left to HR which often has no idea whether or not the new hire will be a good fit with an existing team. It is like an arranged marriage. Managers and their key team members should drive the hiring process. Developing these key new hires should be part of the job description of their teammates with metrics and rewards for a job well done.* [14]

A powerful Management Dynamo keeps the People growing and performing along with your organization's ambitions. Working effectively with each other is often a source of our happiest and most satisfying memories long after the quarterly numbers have been forgotten.

It is equally important to judiciously fire or transfer. "One bad apple spoils the barrel," and one person who is not aligned in skill or with the Culture can retard progress for everyone. You do a person a favor when you guide them to the place where they can contribute with enthusiasm and skill.

[14] Janet Jacobs

ESSENTIALS OF THE PEOPLE DYNAMO

Job Skills	Talent. Technical capability. Competence. Knowledge.
Bandwidth	Time capability. Matches workload. Flexibility to reassign as priorities change.
Experience	Productivity. Effectiveness with minimal supervision. Can train and mentor others.
Maturity	Judgment. Problem solving, critical thinking. Respected.
Advancement	Succession planning, bench strength. Headroom to grow. Readiness for more responsibility.

II. HOW THE 7 DYNAMOS GENERATE ORGANIZATIONAL POWER

ESSENTIALS OF THE RESOURCES DYNAMO

- **Knowledge**
- **Time**
- **Money**
- **Brand**
- **Network**
- **Government Regulations**

7

the resources dynamo

The Resources Dynamo manages relationships with external ecosystems.

Imagine all of the other Dynamos in place and designed to run at top speed. Unless you have enough Resources — money, time, brand recognition, legal rights — the gas tank of your Ferrari is empty.

Without the right Resources, even well-organized ideas won't have enough traction to win the race. For instance, timing is often critical: the date of a new product's release in relationship to the Christmas buying season or model year; meeting investors' expectations on schedule to secure the next round of funding.

The other Dynamos are primarily under internal design control. The Resources Dynamo acknowledges the need to optimize external relationships.

An enterprise exists to earn compensation, in various forms, from others. It operates in a complex array of customer, competitor, investor, regulatory, supply chain, social media, and public perception ecosystems. Flows of money, information, recognition, and government rules must be consciously managed, or wisely adapted to, in harmony with an organization's Purpose. Properly attended to, the Resource Dynamo fills the organization's gas tank so that the whole system can reach the finish line at top speed.

ESSENTIALS OF THE RESOURCES DYNAMO

Knowledge	Intellectual property, trade secrets, industry experience
Time	Lead time, time to market, timing
Money	Investment, revenue, profits, cash
Brand	Reputation, social capital, brand loyalty
Network	Customer relationships, communications channels, supply chains, social media presence
Government Relations	Legal and lobbying resources, response to government regulation, compliance.

> **❝** Make no little plans; they have no magic to stir men's blood."
> **– Daniel Hudson Burnham,**
> *Architect*
> Wikipedia

SECTION III.

HOW TO TURBOCHARGE ORGANIZATIONAL POWER

f you've been reading with a particular organization in mind, it's probably obvious to you where improvements are needed. How do you go about acting on this understanding?

First, ASSESS your Dynamos:

- Bring your key people together to measure the baselines for The 7 Dynamos.
- Is each Dynamo "draining, sustaining, or gaining" organizational power for you?
- Commit to goals that quantify the changes needed.

Then, CHOOSE your Power-Process Tools

- The Power-Process Tools will strengthen Dynamos that are not "gaining" organizational power.
- Engage your team in using these simple, familiar tools to reach your goals.

"A goal is a planned conflict with the status quo." [15]

The status quo has a way of fighting back.

The best way to vanquish it is with an organized plan of attack.

[15] Hyrum W. Smith, founder of the Franklin Quest Company in 1983. Creator of the Franklin Planner.

assess your
dynamos

Even if it seems obvious where improvement is needed, it is tremendously valuable to get your team together to put into words and numbers how much improvement is needed and where. *Make three critical decisions before you meet.*

❑ 1. identify the stakeholders

At a minimum, invite your leadership team. You may also invite some of their key direct reports. Include key team members who may have different perspectives based on their positions and different personality types. The more widely you build awareness of The 7 Dynamos, the more you can engage everyone to help keep them strong.

❑ 2. choose your "conductor"

You, as the Leader, are "the composer" of the music. Your "conductor" is the one who schedules the rehearsals, orders the sheet music, makes sure everyone knows their parts, and keeps the musicians organized to perform together. Delegate this vital role to someone who can help you maintain focus on the process. This role is a leadership development opportunity and a chance to practice managing a strategic initiative.

❑ 3. schedule the meeting(s)

Schedule two meetings, on consecutive days. On the first day, use a white board or shared screen to capture everyone's input. Allow enough time for each Dynamo. On the second day, set goals and choose the Power-Process Tools.

CONDUCTING THE ASSESSMENT

Kick off Meeting 1 by reviewing the Symptoms and Evidence (page 6). How big is the task ahead?

Then, establish the baseline for each Dynamo. Is it *"draining, sustaining, or gaining"* your organizational power? Where, how, and why?

You may find yourselves moving quickly with a high degree of consensus from one Dynamo to the next. Or, you may encounter quite a bit of disagreement. If so, take the time to surface the issues. You will likely find valuable nuggets of information this way. Whether or not you experience a session of "heavy lifting," in which emotionally or politically charged discoveries are voiced, wait until the next day to hold Meeting 2.

Meeting 2 begins with the assessment baselines from the previous day. Decide together where to focus first. Set measurable goals.

Document how you will close the gaps between today's baseline and tomorrow's success metrics for each Dynamo. Your action plan can take the form of a simple checklist, a Gantt chart, or team leaders who are responsible to manage resources and schedule for major projects.

The chart on page 52 will help you choose one or more of the Power-Process Tools. Using them can correct deficiencies in more than one Dynamo at the same time.

Ask your conductor to prepare a plan for following through. The rubber meets the road with deadlines. Realistic due dates and progress reviews along the way help people stay focused and accountable.

As you achieve your success metrics, you will confirm a noticeable difference in organizational power. Your Symptoms and Evidence will shift as you gear up any weak Dynamos.

CHOOSE YOUR POWER-PROCESS TOOLS

These simple tools are most likely familiar to you. They have proven themselves over time in many environments. They add value for both strategic and day-to-day critical thinking and decision making.

I call them Power-Process Tools as a reminder that they are more effective when you follow a disciplined process as you use them.

The 8 Power-Process Tools strengthen the Dynamos by

- Fostering collaboration
- Integrating functional plans
- Reinforcing discipline and accountability
- Producing more robust outcomes

They add immediate value by

- Giving people the experience of quality decision-making
- Generating shared mental models with visual output
- Torpedoing politics

power-process tool	when to use
1. **Power Meeting Process**	Start immediately to unlock people's energy, enthusiasm
2. **Business Process Mapping**	Clarify roles and responsibilities to eliminate wasted time and effort
3. **Ultimate Policy Deployment**	Get everyone "pulling together" towards bold strategic goals
4. **Cross-Functional Teams**	Solve thorny problems, develop products faster, manage strategic initiatives
5. **Illuminating Roadmaps**	Visually integrate functional milestones across time
6. **People Capability Blueprints**	Build people who are ready for your future
7. **Water-Tight Problem Solving**	Plug the leaks with 8D, DMAIC, FMEA
8. **Quality Decision Making**	Better process, better outcomes

❶
power meeting process

If you use only one Power-Process Tool, make it this one.

Raising the quality of your meetings immediately builds organizational power. The ***Power Meeting Process*** saves time and encourages better decision making.

"To meet" is an action verb. To meet with power is to unlock people's enthusiasm and ability to achieve clearly defined outcomes, in meetings requiring 2 people or 200 people.

People look forward to meetings they know will be run well. They appreciate the chance to participate in making important decisions, to learn important information, and to help to solve a serious problem.

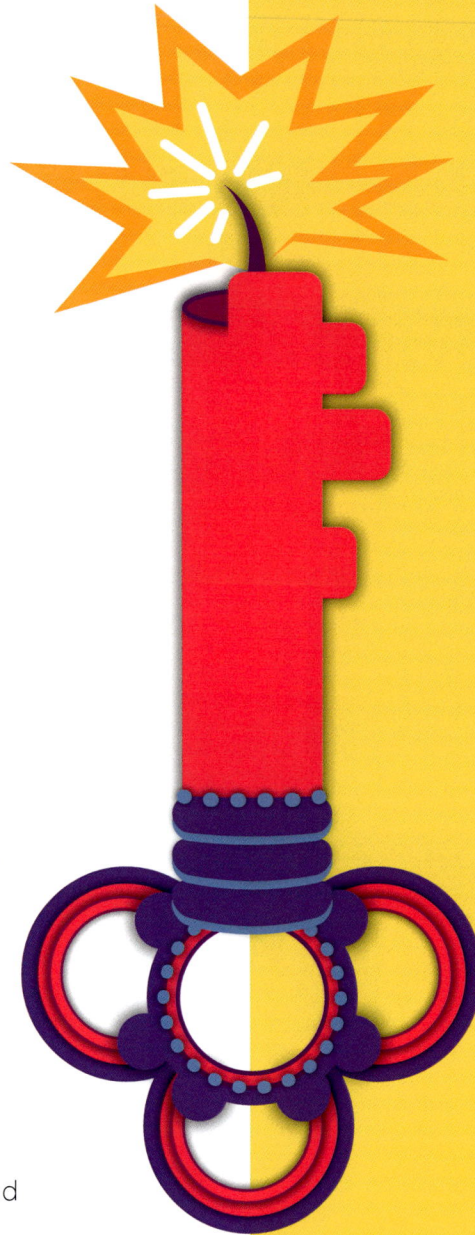

MEETING TYPES

Meetings come in 7 basic flavors, each with its own preparation, pacing, and structure. The agenda for one meeting can include several different types — for example, begin with 15 minutes of "information sharing," invest 30 minutes in "problem solving," and wrap up with 10 minutes of "planning" to recap action items and timing, define content for next meeting, etc.

MEETING TYPE	PURPOSE / DESCRIPTION
1. Informational	Helps people align their actions outside of the meeting by giving and getting information, status, changes
2. Decision-Making	Identifies needed decisions, generates choices, understands consequences, reaches consensus on a plan of action
3. Brainstorming	Non-judgmentally generating ideas and options, unlocking creative thinking, broadening scope and approach
4. Problem Solving	Identifying problems, specifying action steps with owners and timeline
5. Planning	Creating an objective or goal, specifying the present situation, outlining an implementation plan
6. Opportunity Capture	Identifying opportunities, prioritizing, specifying action steps
7. Working Session	Setting aside time for people to work together on a project that is hard to find time for during the regular work day

PLANNING AND RUNNING THE MEETING

Step 1: Define the Purpose

❑ Verbalize the outcome – what will this meeting achieve?

❑ Put it in writing – on a slide or a white board or in the invitation.

Example: "By the end of this meeting we will accomplish..."

❑ Confirm with the Participants.

Step 2: Design the Meeting

❑ Type - clarify the meeting type(s) you will use to achieve the outcome.

Specialized meetings (FMEA, Ultimate Policy Deployment, BPM) require additional prep/tools.

❑ Participants – identify who must attend, and invite only them.

❑ Agenda – draft the content and sequence.

❑ Pre-Work – identify any preparation required.

❑ Timing – allow enough time before the meeting to accomplish the pre-work and enough time in the meeting for consensus decision making, Q&A, or understanding and alignment.

❑ Location – reserve space and/or the call-in system.

❑ Logistics – follow a checklist for large meetings or offsites.

Step 3: Follow the Process

❑ **Send** invitations that include the purpose/outcomes, date & time, location, Participants, and pre-work.

❑ **Confirm** that Participants can and will attend.

Step 4: Lead the Meeting

❑ **Follow** the flow chart.

❑ **Choose** a timekeeper – stay on time to the Agenda.

❑ **Choose** a scribe to write Decisions and Actions so they are visible to all in real time.

❑ **Use** any or all of these tools:

- Consensus
- Roles & responsibilities
- Strawman
- Decision making framework
- TQM tools
- Decisions and Action Items tracking

Step 5: Rate the meeting

Ask each Participant to give their numerical score; write on a white board what worked and what didn't. Use this information to improve the next meeting.

MEETING
flowchart

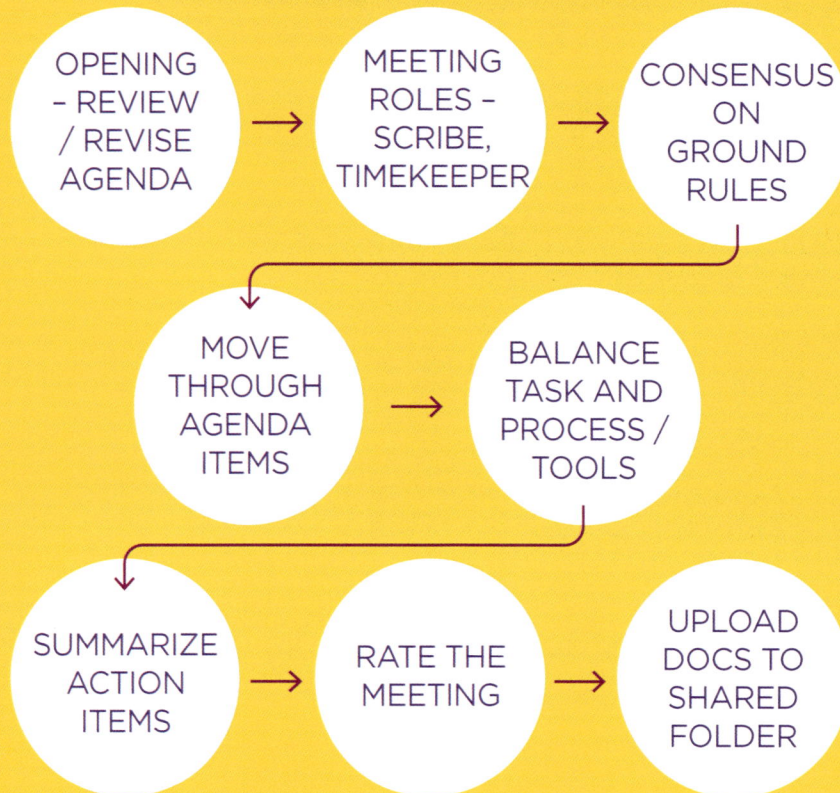

OPENING – REVIEW / REVISE AGENDA → MEETING ROLES – SCRIBE, TIMEKEEPER → CONSENSUS ON GROUND RULES

MOVE THROUGH AGENDA ITEMS → BALANCE TASK AND PROCESS / TOOLS

SUMMARIZE ACTION ITEMS → RATE THE MEETING → UPLOAD DOCS TO SHARED FOLDER

Do you really need "Minutes?"

Unless it's required (e.g., corporate board meetings), they are often not worth the effort. It can be just as effective to publish a running list of Decisions and review the Action Items at every meeting.

MEETING GROUND RULES

- Be on time: start and stop on time

- Show up or inform meeting leader; ask if sending a rep is appropriate

- Turn phones to "silent" or "vibrate"

- One person speaks at a time; no sidebar conversations

- Manage to the agenda; track important but off-topic items in a "parking lot"

- Focus on issues, not on people

- Come prepared

- Respectful interaction: listen, talk, challenge respectfully

- Pay attention and participate; stay topic-focused

CONFERENCE CALL COURTESY

- Be aware of time differences when scheduling meetings

- Provide dial-in numbers on your meeting invitation (and/or conference system access)

- Make materials accessible; double-check their availability in advance

- Place conference phone away from papers and noises

- Speak loudly enough so that ALL can hear what's being said

- Regularly check in with phone (invisible) participants

- Translate non-verbal signals (nodding heads, smiles) for the phone participants

- Remember: more than one conversation sounds like NOISE to those on the phone

2
business process mapping

Nothing builds clarity and efficiency for day-to-day work as powerfully as cross-functional business process mapping.

Business *Process Maps* define the phases, the deliverables, and the functional "swim lanes" which work together to provide the outcomes. It is a "high effort, high impact" exercise.

THE PHASES [16]

1. **Prep Phase**

   Deliverables: The business process owner drafts the Problem Statement, Goal Statement, Block Diagram (scope)

2. **Plan Phase**

   Deliverables: Heads of Departments confirm Problem Statement, Goal Statement, Block Diagram, their Mappers, the face-to-face mapping location, and Visio Master

3. **Map "As Is" Phase**

   Deliverables: Heads of Departments take ownership of the root causes of the Problem Statement which the Mappers identify in the current business process and illustrate in Visio.

4. **Map "To Be" Phase**

   Deliverables: Heads of Department accept the Mappers' recommendations to correct the root causes by implementing the new business process.

5. **Implement and Sustain Phase**

   Deliverables: The business process owner and the mappers document, communicate, train, "go live," measure process metrics and reconvene to make any necessary adjustments on an ongoing basis.

[16] The "Business Process Map for Business Process Mapping" (BPM for BPM") is available in pdf form at www.7dynamos.com

THE ROLES

Executive Sponsor:

- Ensures organizational buy-in and support of the changes
- Provides or advocates for resources

HOD (Head of Department)

- Assigns and supports the Mapper from their functional area
- Participates in phase-end reviews
- Commits to support implementation of process changes

BPM Owner

- The functional department head who leads the BPM process
- Oversees the mapping team during the "As Is" and "To Be" Phases
- Is responsible for Phase 5 (Implement and Sustain) on an ongoing basis

Lead Mapper

- May be selected from among the Mappers
- Schedules meetings and manages logistics and communications
- Is the primary interface with the Visio Master
- Maintains the Parking Lot, Issues and Recommendations Log, and other documents
- Communicates status to the BPM Owner; requests help in resolving issues

Mappers

- Work face-to-face together "at the wall" to define the "As Is" process, diagnose the issues and root causes, and then design the "To Be" process with corrective actions
- Plan the implementation

Visio Master

- Transcribes the on-the-wall process maps to illustrate the root causes and corrective actions

Facilitator

- Provides BPM training and guidance, mapping standards
- Facilitates meetings as needed

3 ultimate policy deployment

Ultimate Policy Deployment _is the master Power-Process Tool because it simultaneously corrects a multitude of organizational power deficiencies._

t demands high effort. In return, it delivers the highest impact of all the Power-Process Tools.

Ultimate Policy Deployment commands unified action by the whole organization towards the bigger picture. Instead of the boss "pushing" people, it gets everyone "pulling together" towards bold strategic goals. It aligns everyone on "the vital few" actions, which are integrated into the organization's day-to-day work (so they actually get done).

Janet Jacobs, president of Anchor Audio and Discount Audio for more than a decade, had this observation about the failure of most strategic planning processes to deliver meaningful change:

> *"Too many corporations (especially the multibillion-dollar versions) write an annual strategic plan, or pay to have a consulting firm create the plan, and the management team throws it in a drawer. Buy-in from the team is critical. Reinforcement of the deliverables needs to be constant, and the Leader must be hands on to keep the team on track. The strategic plan is not static. It must change as new information is pulled into the decision-making process. This is the hallmark of a true leader. They make decisions constantly to continue forward momentum. They do not wring their hands and constantly request more information."* [17]

Hoshin Kanri originated at Toyota in the 1970's and came to the United States as Policy Deployment. The name makes sense if you think of Policy = Strategy, and Deployment = Action. Policies are decisions; "we will do this; we will not do that." Ultimate Policy Deployment puts strategy into action with visual clarity.

Excellent books have been published about Hoshin Kanri in its full breadth and depth. It's always an option to do it that way. However, I have seen outstanding results from this accelerated approach, which adds a few special ingredients, and I recommend it for its immediate clarity and simplicity.

---

[17] Janet Jacobs, President of Anchor Audio and Discount Audio, 2007-2017

ULTIMATE POLICY DEPLOYMENT HAS 6 STEPS:

1. **X-Matrix**

Upper management kicks off the X-Matrix by presenting breakthrough goals and validating them with the leadership team

Special ingredient: *The Leader presents ambitious goals that are exciting but may seem unattainable, generating doubt and negativity ("Sounds great, but I'm thinking of all the reasons we can't do it.").*

Annual Goals	Revenue	Profitability	Market Share	Customer Satisfaction	Operating Costs	Strategic Initiatives		Targets		Initiatiive Owners	
						Changes in how we do things					
						Initiatives / Annual Goals / Targets / Breakthrough Objectives					
						Revenue	Milestone Date		Name Name Name Name Name		
						Profitability					
						Market Share					
						Market Capitalization					
						Breakthrough Goals					

2. **SWOT**

The team immediately conducts a good-old-fashioned SWOT analysis (to capture all of their "but we can't get there because" doubts) and organizes the responses into an affinity diagram

Special ingredients: Everyone uses yellow 3" square Post-it Notes® and black Sharpies® to "anonymize" responses. Ten minutes of absolute silence prevail while people write their S, W, O, and T's and put them on the wall. Teams of two organize each category into themes.

3. **Priorities**

The team "votes" on the themes to uncover the consensus priorities

Special ingredient: Everyone has 3 green dots (votes), so it only takes a couple of minutes to reveal the team's priorities. These become the Initiatives on the X-Matrix.

4. **Initiatives**

Each Initiative gets an Initiative Leader.

Special ingredient: Qualifications for Initiative Leader go beyond being an obvious subject matter expert to include leadership and facilitation skills, readiness for a development opportunity.

5. Scope, Team and Timeline:

Initiative Leaders use a one-page Initiative Template to define a robust problem statement, success metrics, approach, milestones, and team members

Special ingredient: *Only people with "real work to be done" are on the team.*

Initiative Template

Initiative Name	
Leader	
Robust Problem Statement	Symptoms we experience and their quantified business impact.
SMART Goal(s) and Success Metrics	S.M.A.R.T. Goals Success Criteria (e.g., X% improvement on Y metric by Z time
Scope / Approach "the work to be done"	E.g., sites, products, departments, stakeholders Sequence of events (e.g., gather data, analyze, recommend, fund, communicate)
Milestones	1. Deliverable and date 2. Deliverable and date 3. Deliverable and date 4. Deliverable and date

	Core Team Member	Function / Department	Role on Team ("real work" to be done)
1	Name		Leader
2	Name		Analyze and recommend plan by XX department
3	Name		Voice of XXX when making tradeoffs
4	Name		Represent interests of Department XXX
5	Name		

6.   Accountability

Regular reviews guarantee progress and accountability as milestones are met

Special ingredient: *Within 30 days, Initiative Leaders present their Templates to the full Ultimate Policy Deployment team to be sure the spirit of everyone's Post-it Notes® will be addressed. Milestone reviews drive ongoing accountability to the schedule.*

4

cross-functional teams

Almost all strategic change requires the collaboration of more than one function.

F ormally engaging a **Cross-functional Team** creates the Structure and Process for the functions to make tradeoffs and strategic decisions and manage the schedule together. Where there may have been functional "silos" or a blame culture, chartering cross-

functional teams to focus on a deliverable bigger than any one of them sets the stage for collaboration.

Great teams are rare. Why? Because they are a mini-version of a powerful organization with the same 7 Dynamos. High performing cross-functional teams contribute to an organization's bench strength by developing general management and leadership skills. They strengthen the Culture, as People rise to each other's expectations, and the passion for excellence is contagious.

My greatly esteemed colleague, Jane Creech,[18] is the premier authority on high performing teams. She confirms that people who have been on such teams remember them as thrilling and defining times in their lives.

A basic checklist for launching successful Cross-Functional Teams:

- ❏ **Establish** the clear outcomes the team must deliver and by when
- ❏ **Define** the decision-making boundaries and authority
- ❏ **Select** no more than 5 core team members
- ❏ **Make sure** only members with real work to do are on the team
- ❏ **Identify** a leader with adequate organization and facilitation skills
- ❏ **Enlist** the right executive sponsor
- ❏ **Establish** clear roles & responsibilities
- ❏ **Reach consensus** on meeting frequency and duration
- ❏ **Set** behavioral norms and ground rules
- ❏ **Decide** how the team will reach consensus and manage conflict
- ❏ **Choose** your decision process, guiding principles, and roles
- ❏ **Set** communication expectations within and outside the team

[18] Jane Creech, catalyst for cross-functional collaboration, is also an Executive Education Lecturer for the Haas School of Business at UC Berkeley. https://strategicbizsys.com

5

illuminating roadmaps

Roadmaps are a familiar tool; turbocharge yours with a collaborative development process.

Build a visual timeline which establishes a clear starting point and the path to your success metrics. Everyone will be able to understand and better manage their interdependencies.

Roadmap Execution Confidence Assessment

Sample Milestones – aligned objectives and metrics

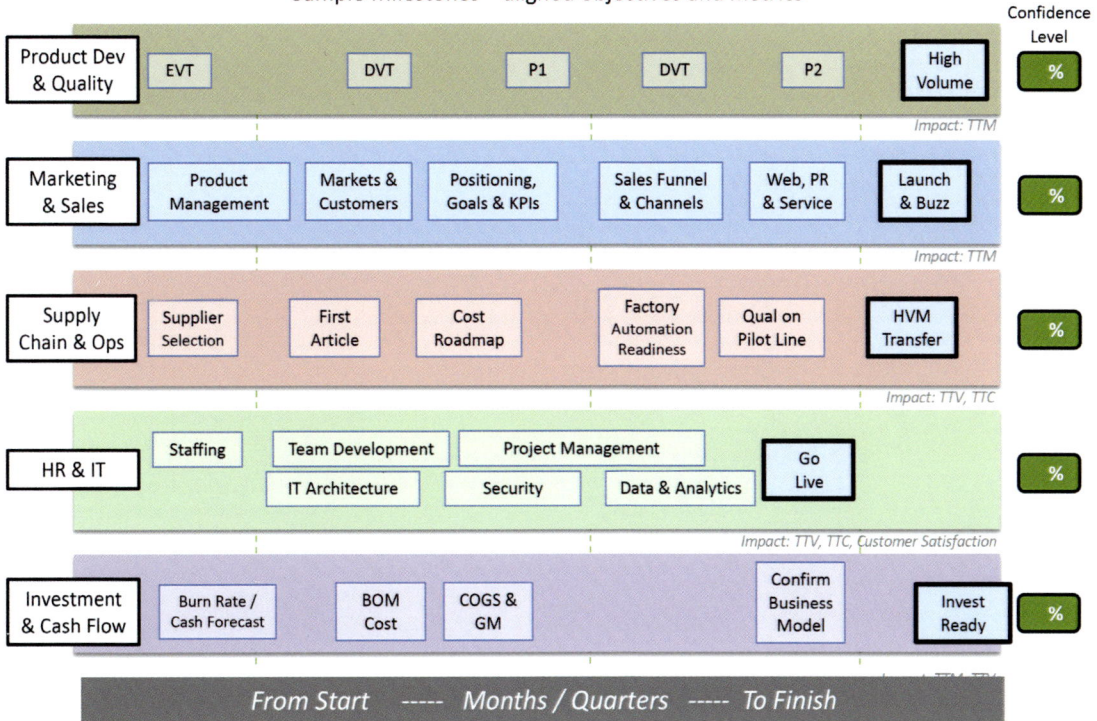

							Confidence Level
Product Dev & Quality	EVT	DVT	P1	DVT	P2	High Volume	%

Impact: TTM

Marketing & Sales	Product Management	Markets & Customers	Positioning, Goals & KPIs	Sales Funnel & Channels	Web, PR & Service	Launch & Buzz	%

Impact: TTM

Supply Chain & Ops	Supplier Selection	First Article	Cost Roadmap	Factory Automation Readiness	Qual on Pilot Line	HVM Transfer	%

Impact: TTV, TTC

HR & IT	Staffing	Team Development / IT Architecture	Project Management / Security	Data & Analytics	Go Live	%

Impact: TTV, TTC, Customer Satisfaction

Investment & Cash Flow	Burn Rate / Cash Forecast	BOM Cost	COGS & GM	Confirm Business Model	Invest Ready	%

From Start ----- Months / Quarters ----- To Finish

6

people capability blueprints

This visual tool is used to establish a clear plan for putting future capability in place.

"Bubble charts" are customized for the needs of specific departments or organizations.

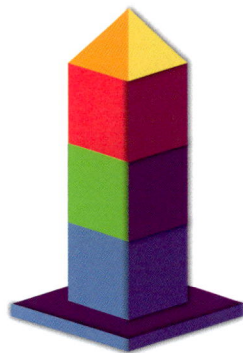

They are illustrated on a two-axis chart, where each individual is represented by a "bubble" which may need to move up and/or forward in capability to meet the organization's future needs.

The exercise might include all of the people in a technical department or a satellite office or a group of high-potential individuals.

Here are the steps: [19]

1. **Establish** the future needs based on your expectation of a changing mission

2. **Define** the skills and/or capabilities that will be needed in granular scale

3. **Assess** each individual's baseline position (bubble)

4. **Evaluate** each person's potential to grow into the needed roles / capabilities

5. **Plan** how to offer each person development opportunities, or a transfer or termination, along with needs for new hires

[19] A "How To" guide can be found at www.7dynamos.com.

Example

Current Org

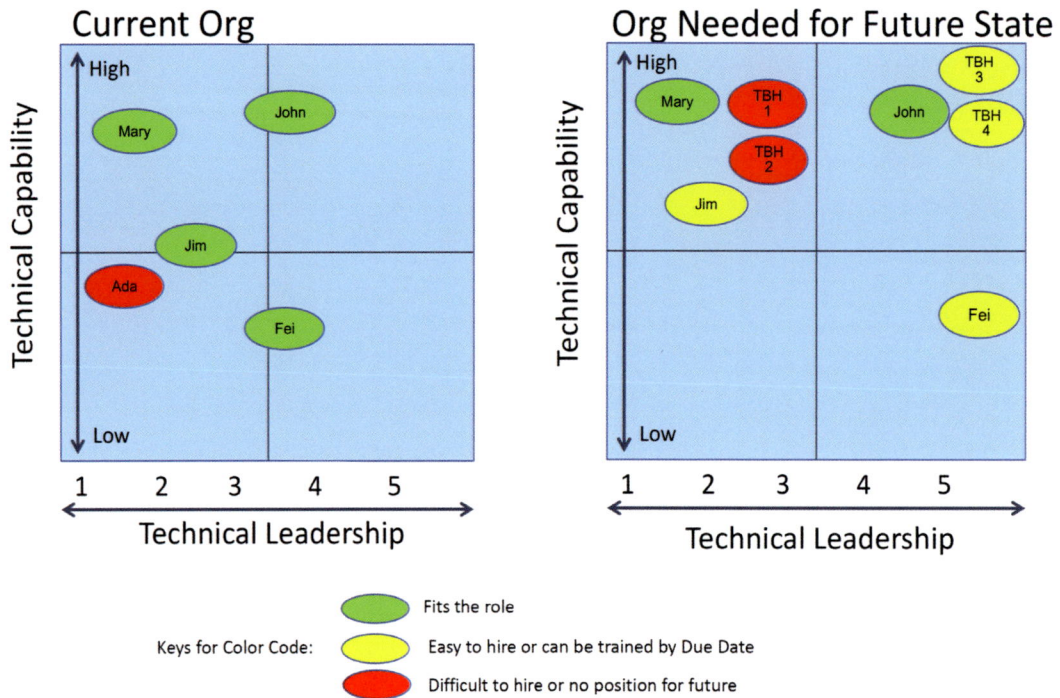

Technical Capability

High

Mary

John

Jim

Ada

Fei

Low

1 2 3 4 5

Technical Leadership

Org Needed for Future State

Technical Capability

High

Mary

TBH 1

TBH 2

Jim

TBH 3

John

TBH 4

Fei

Low

1 2 3 4 5

Technical Leadership

Keys for Color Code:

Fits the role

Easy to hire or can be trained by Due Date

Difficult to hire or no position for future

In this example, the organization knows it will need stronger technical capability and additional bandwidth in the future. The capability can partly be developed by training the existing People, but new hires will also be needed.

7

water-tight problem solving

Powerful organizations develop and practice a disciplined approach to quickly and accurately solving problems.

The most important and widely used problem solving tool is the **8 Disciplines.** Developed by Ford Motor Company in the 1980s, the "8D's" is a recipe for accurately identifying root causes and taking the right corrective actions to prevent problems from recurring. If you aren't using this tool with great fervor, you are missing a chance to plug the leaks in your organizational power.

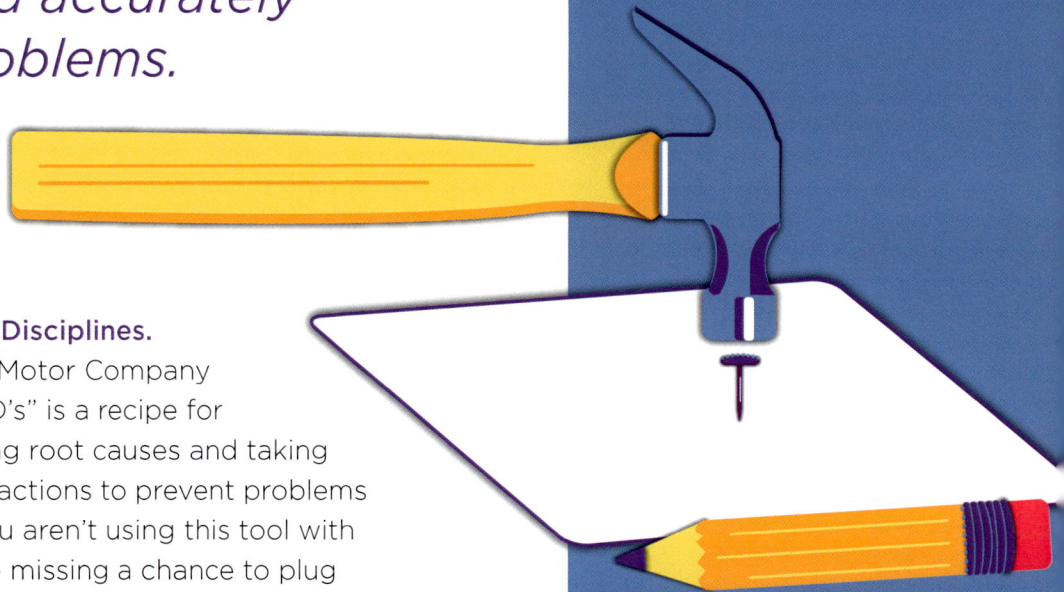

THE 8 DISCIPLINES

0.	**Awareness** of the problem	
1.	**Form** the team	
2.	**Define** the problem	
3.	**Contain** the problem	
4.	**Determine** root cause	
5.	**Validate** corrective action	
6.	**Implement** corrective action	
7.	**Prevent** recurrence	
8.	**Congratulate** and adjourn the team	

A similar process, frequently used by engineering departments, is **DMAIC:** Define, Measure, Analyze, Improve, Control. [20]

More powerful is the higher effort, higher impact **FMEA** (Failure Modes and Effects Analysis). [21]

You can find extensive resources on line for using these problem-solving tools. Whichever you choose, using them consistently will have a transformative effect not only on your Culture Dynamo, but your organization's performance and reputation.

[20] https://en.wikipedia.org/wiki/DMAIC

[21] https://en.wikipedia.org/wiki/Failure_mode_and_effects_analysis

8

quality decision making

No one can definitively control the outcome of a decision, but we can control the quality of our decision-making process.

Use all four of these **Quality Decision Making** tools to make better quality decisions.

A. EFFORT/IMPACT MATRIX

For prioritizing This simple Power-Process Tool will clearly reveal the low-hanging fruit and where more analysis is required to justify investment in bigger bang-for-the-buck projects.

> *"I have seen the biggest success in evaluating and trimming product portfolios and development projects. Eliminating sub-par projects allows the team to lean into critical projects and reduce the time to achieve deliverables."* [22]

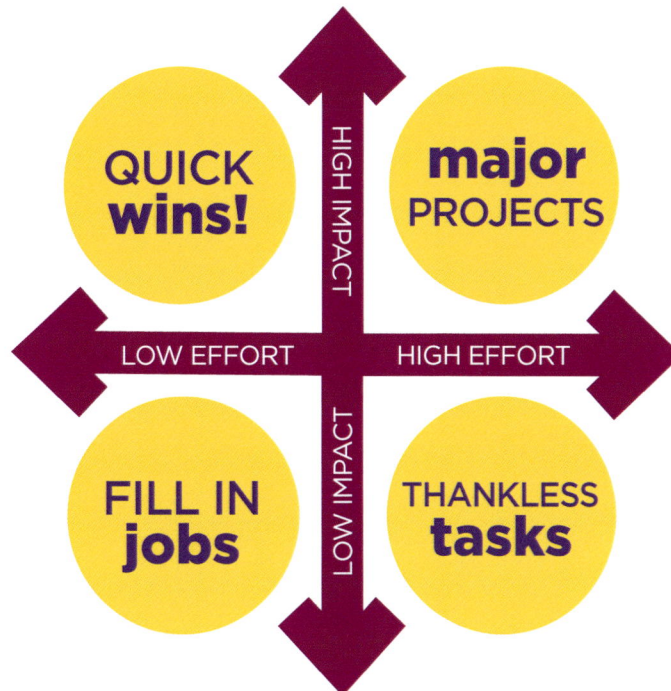

QUICK **wins!**

major PROJECTS

HIGH IMPACT

LOW EFFORT   HIGH EFFORT

LOW IMPACT

FILL IN jobs

THANKLESS **tasks**

---

[22] Janet Jacobs

B. GUIDING PRINCIPLES

To drive alignment When you establish Guiding Principles in advance, it helps people consistently reach consensus on actions that align with strategic Purpose.

Guiding Principles can be simple and general:

- Transparency

- Collaboration

- Teamwork

- Consensus

Or, they can be quite specific: [23]

As a unified team, we agree to

1. Openly share engineering data without reservation

2. Debate and strive to reach consensus or escalate

3. Communicate as one voice

4. Include statements of risk with shared data and conclusions

5. Let others know when we share their data

6. Respect the defined roles and responsibilities, especially across functions

7. Take ownership for making and communicating key decisions within our functional area

8. Assess and communicate impact to the product and to other stakeholders when initiating change

9. Celebrate our success!

---

[23] Client example

C. STEPS IN DECISION MAKING

When choosing among alternatives Resist the urge to plunge in and do the obvious. Follow a disciplined process (it doesn't have to take much time) to assure objectivity and buy-in from the start.

1. Frame the decision	What are we deciding? Not deciding?
2. Set criteria and weight them	What requirements must the solution meet? Are some more important?
3. Generate potential solution options	Include the "as is" option (no change)
4. Rate and rank each option according to the criteria	Which one gets the most "points?"
5. Do a risk assessment on "the winner"	Evaluate likelihood and impact of risks / tradeoffs
6. Confirm or modify the decision / recommendation	Get approvals and funding as needed
7. Create the communication message and plan	Who communicates? What stakeholders are impacted? "Go live" date?
8. Communicate the decision	Collect and accommodate feedback as needed
9. Evaluate and share lessons learned	Improve decision making skills for faster and higher quality next time

D. FRAMING TEMPLATE

When presenting recommendations for approval Follow these steps to present the results of a decision-making process. Note that the recommendation is not revealed until Step 4.

❑ **1. Relevance**

Why is what I am about to present to you important?
How does it relate to our goals or deliverables?

❑ **2. The Issue or Opportunity**

A concise statement

❑ **3. What you Need**

Decision today? Approval for next step? Discussion or input? Other?

❑ **4. Recommendation**

What you are proposing

❑ **5. Implications or Risks**

What it will mean in terms of workload, support, assistance, investment, etc., and any areas that will need risk-mitigation plans

❑ **6. Alternatives You Considered**

Briefly why each is less desirable or effective a solution

❑ **7. Call for Action**

Guide the process until the group is either ready to decide, needs clarification, needs more information, or has alternative recommendations to propose

> **"** There is no winning without pride...Pride is all about caring. It is the sense of pleasure or satisfaction you take in what you do."
>
> **– Jack Stack**
> *The Great Game of Business,* 1992

WHY ORGANIZATIONAL POWER MATTERS

Leading an organization with the power to achieve ambitious goals is deeply rewarding. We want to design and build powerful organizations, of all kinds, because it is exciting to work with colleagues to create great value for our customers.

We do it because we are driven to unlock potential.

And because we love to share a sense of accomplishment with others.

Because it challenges us to be our best and give of our best to others.

In a matter of months, by understanding The 7 Dynamos of Organizational Power, we can transform our organizations.

It is well worth investing the time and effort to mentor our teams in understanding and turbocharging The 7 Dynamos of Organizational Power.

It is simple, though not always easy. We can get going immediately and see results right away. Ideas can turn on a dime. Don't wait.

WEB SITE RESOURCES

The web site **www.7dynamos.com** has

- Customized Consulting

- Success Stories

- Bibliography

- Other Resources

acknowledgements

I am grateful to all of my friends and colleagues whose example and conversations have helped me discover and apply The 7 Dynamos.

Vince Mastropietro, thank you for providing the catalytic environment where The 7 Dynamos coalesced, and for the privilege of supporting the remarkable organizational transformation you led.

Jane Creech, thank you for the crucial concept of Structure and Process on our way back from chartering high-performing teams in Penang.

Maureen Klatt, thank you for verbalizing that "leadership is a job" and for knowledgeably adopting and proliferating the tools.

Attila Lengyel, thank you for the satisfying clang of hearing that last Dynamo drop into place.

Janet and David Jacobs, thank you for your gifted role modeling and our many insightful conversations.

John Backer, thank you for sharpening my thinking with your superb commitment to clarity.

Hazel Wright, thank you for your partnership in validating the tools "in the real world."

Juli Miller, thank you for your unflagging encouragement and critical thinking from the beginning.

Eternal thanks to my guiding lights of genius and foresight, George Friedman, George Gilder, and Arthur M. Young.

about the author

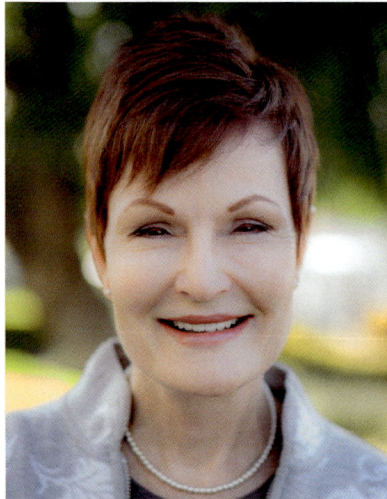

Colleen Cayes supports Leaders who want to build powerful organizations through her **boldlygo** consulting. *The 7 Dynamos of Organizational Power* is the essential framework she has identified for building an organization capable of fulfilling an ambitious vision and accelerating its growth, profitability, and industry leadership.

Colleen was a founding member of the management team at Conner Peripherals, the fastest growing company in American history in 1987. She specializes in structuring complex projects and leading large, multi-functional teams to execute rapidly and efficiently. Her achievements include the rapid ramp up of multi-million-dollar factories in Asia, a guerilla campaign to win $8 million in corporate funding for a revolutionary new product, institutionalizing new technical teams for product reliability and supplier maturity, and revamping the market and technology strategy for a new business unit. Colleen has founded several companies; turned around a Teamster-organized machine shop; and led strategic initiatives within diverse business models ranging from cut flower imports from South America to oil spill contingency plans for the Trans-Alaska Pipeline. She earned her B.A. at Stanford University and her MBA from Harvard. She lives in Utah.

www.7dynamos.com | **colleen@7dynamos.com** | **(505) 603-8003**